Wildness
Before Something
Sublime

COPPER
CANYON
PRESS
REVIEW COPY
NOT FOR RESALE
publicity@coppercanyonpress.org

ALSO BY LEILA CHATTI

Figment

The Mothers (with Dorianne Laux)

Deluge

Ebb

Tunsiya/Amrikiya

Wildness Before Something Sublime

LEILA CHATTI

COPPER CANYON PRESS

PORT TOWNSEND, WASHINGTON

Cover art: Laura Makabresku, *Untitled*, 2024

Photographs included in the poem "Examination of Night" are courtesy of the author.

Copper Canyon Press is in residence at Fort Worden State Park in Port Townsend, Washington, under the auspices of Centrum. Centrum is a gathering place for artists and creative thinkers from around the world, students of all ages and backgrounds, and audiences seeking extraordinary cultural enrichment.

LIBRARY OF CONGRESS CATALOGING-IN-PUBLICATION DATA
Names: Chatti, Leila, 1990– author
Title: Wildness before something sublime / Leila Chatti.
Description: Port Townsend, Washington : Copper Canyon Press, 2025. |
    Summary: "A collection of poems by Leila Chatti"— Provided by
    publisher.
Identifiers: LCCN 2025021581 (print) | LCCN 2025021582 (ebook) |
    ISBN 9781556597169 paperback | ISBN 9781619323162 epub
Subjects: LCGFT: Poetry
Classification: LCC PS3603.H37978 W55 2025 (print) |
    LCC PS3603.H37978 (ebook) | DDC 811/.6—dc23/eng/20250523
LC record available at https://lccn.loc.gov/2025021581
LC ebook record available at https://lccn.loc.gov/2025021582

9 8 7 6 5 4 3 2 FIRST PRINTING

COPPER CANYON PRESS
Post Office Box 271
Port Townsend, Washington 98368
www.coppercanyonpress.org

for Naïma

have loved

whom I love

will love

beyond time, beyond language

[I:] I feel that I must speak to you. Why do you not let me sleep,

as I am tired? I feel that the disturbance comes from you.

What induces you to keep me awake?

[Soul:] Now is no time to sleep, but you should be awake and prepare

important matters in nocturnal work. The great work begins.

Carl Jung

And this business of writing. I see through a mirror, in the dark.

Alejandra Pizarnik

CONTENTS

NIGHT POEMS

AFTER THOUGHT

SHADOW/SELF

AUTHOR'S NOTE

This book was written when I wasn't writing. This is what I said, anyway—*I'm not writing.* Yet, of course, these poems exist.

I think of myself as having *discovered* these poems rather than having wrought them—I am the one who held the rod, entered the field, but I did not conjure the water already there. I feel they are cowritten: some in conversation with another (unaware) writer, others a dictation of a voice beyond my understanding—my unconscious or an external force—call it God, the Muse, I can't say, but I know better than to claim it as mine alone. Call it divine.

The poems in "Oracle" are written as echoes or shadow sides—responses, negative images—to poems by women whose voices first led me to discover my own. Each poem in "Divine" was written while flipping very quickly, at random, through beloved books and recording words and fragments that evoked a bodily response or otherwise snared my attention, as well as my misreadings, reactions, and associative leaps. The "Night Poems" were written on the brink of sleep, on my cell phone. Often, I would doze off midway through. The final sections, "After Thought" and "Shadow/Self," are the poems that arrived once I learned again, at last, how to move out of my mind's way.

Wildness
Before Something
Sublime

ORACLE

IN THE NIGHT MANY VOICES

a cento

All night long I am. Night-voiced. Bruising, these night mists. In darkness the world is. What my body touches. An eye, not of the body, keeps watch. The dreaming houses all snuff out. Both leaf and leaf-shadow. Moon-plumaged. A thousand silences. In the proliferation and cancellation of words. A great snow, the gliding emptiness. Starred with words, let night bless that. Let the night enter. My night mind sees such strange happenings. My hours married to shadow. Braver at night. A little rip in the mind. I speak the way I speak inside. Let me speak it in a whisper. On the wall, a corresponding figure links me to the darkness I cannot control. Night goes on forever inside. Not in the real world, but in the buried one. I see no thing other than myself. I forgive my mind. Darkness without brevity. Its dream, the vanishing point. Night filling the field, and making it. So near night I couldn't tell. I lie still. As an invitation. Of some suffering, but quietly. Asked the night for help, and some help came. On the eyes black sleep. My dreams not far away. I could see obscurity's own kind of brilliance. I am the one who sees and does not see. For years I have opened my eyes and not known. Where I was, I saw myself. In the dark window. Wordless, the pure receptacle. I am not supposed to turn away. What is still inside settles down for the darkness I listen to. Long dark. Something dark and endlessly. Open, like a child's damp hand in sleep. Each star a word. *Cataclysm, vertiginous, forever.* What I was and what I become. When one is no longer emerging one is. Vanishing. I'm being dreamt. There I am, a secret. Of my own. This name no one answers to. Far and close at once. What breaks is night. Where it touches me I vanish. Night, the divine, crosses the room. Through. The word and the window. The still night drifts, deep, like snow. Snow, life, always in the present tense. Night I am never done with. Black against the white space of the mind. Sky. Like an open well.

ONE WOMAN
A Poem Unvoiced

after Sylvia Plath

I have had my fate. I have idled and idled.
I have plucked death from me like a common bone,
And run carelessly, assuredly, like something common.
I have tried not to feel too soft. I have tried to be preternatural.
I have tried to be discerning in hatred, like men,
Discerning in public streets, with the worthless watchful bitter many,
Groping, through thin light, for the body of no one.

I was ready. The black sky flattening
Above was crushing me in place.
I was ready.
I had no shame.
I felt I could admit the origin—
It was time. It was time, and the body
Stopped raveling itself with inattention, as if I were unprepared.

I am wild. I am wild. It is the wildness before something sublime:
The violet hour after the earth stills, when the roots
Bury their tails, their suffusion. It is so raucous, elsewhere.
The shades, the bodies, are black and moving, like infinity.
Silence approaches and swells. Its invisible clarity
Swells, ink opening to let stillness in.
It erases knowledge, languageless.

A weakness is withering within me, a new fragility.
I am sutured together like the universe. There is this whiteness,
This ewe of whiteness. I unfurl my soles on a sea.
The water is thin. It is thin with this idleness.
I am untouched. I am stilled out of touch.
My ears are relieved by this whiteness.
I hear everything.

IN LAMENT OF MY UTERUS

after Anne Sexton

No one in me is a bird.
All my wings have stilled.
They wanted to leave you in
but they will not.
They said you were measurably full
and must be emptied.
They said you were resilient, remediable,
but they were wrong.
You are shrieking like an infant.
You and I are torn.

Foul void,
in lament of the woman I am
and of the body of the woman I am
and of the nugatory creator and its disappointments
I shriek for you. I despair to live.
Be gone, flesh. Be gone, ichor.
Release, reveal. Reveal that which will not hold.
Be gone to the muck of the fallow.
Farewell, seeds.

Each cell has a death.
There is nothing here, uninhabitable.
It is not enough, no good.
No person, no one, wants to need, to speak of it.
It is misery this year that I must uproot finally
and forget the dream of yielding.
A blessing had been promised and did not arrive.
Many women are shrieking, alone, with this:
one is in an MRI's throat cursing the machine,
one is in the dirt rending a weed,
one is fording a dull season of grief,

one is on a corner imploring,
one is slaughtering a lamb and thinking of God,
one is straddling her hand in Malmö,
one is sluicing dust from marble in Tunis,
one is stripping her walls the color of a moonless night,
one is convalescing (having been swiftly broken),
one is fetal on the floor in Santa Fe,
one is wiping a trickle of gore from her thigh,
one is staring in a mirror of a room
at the edge of the sea and one is
anywhere and some are everywhere and all
seem to be screaming, although some cannot
utter a sound.

Sanguine burden,
in lament of the woman I am
I relinquish my ten-foot shawl,
I contemn my useless youth,
I destroy the vessel of suffering
(as that is my part).
I snub the sentimental organ,
I dismiss the amorphous proximity of heaven,
I spit thorns
(as that is my part).
I figure nothing certain but tribulation
(as that is my part).
For this thing the body denies
let me shriek
for the deserted,
for the aching,
for the unwriteable wrong—
no!

CHILDLESS WOMAN

after Sylvia Plath

A year and still this womb-
dark silence I grope through, moon-
cold tile I pad alone. In other houses, children go

on sleeping. Mothers do not stir. Rosy lines
in the window, dawn crossing the room like a daughter into bed. Here, a knot
of shadow unfurls in water. Again I analyze its threads. I hold myself

accountable; then, at a distance. Achieve
nothing but grief. Wash in a haze again my body,
the lights off and ivory

towels in the closet, stark as a shriek.
A year of days passed like mirrors;
in each one, myself, brutally unchanged. Unbidden as an image

rising in the mind, rag of cloud and blood-
punctual sun. Morning humiliation-red.
Grim trail through no forest

I vanish behind me, drops measured as a funeral
cortege. Hours on my knees, of this—
until I slip back into sheets, dreams blank as corpses.

LOST BABY POEM

after Lucille Clifton

You would have been born in winter.
Like a shadow, the year of dark
began with the body and reached
beyond. The calendar of no

time, dayless, panes and panes of gray.
You would have been born in winter.
Now only a chill sleeps inside
my bones. Each breath shivers, silver,

my living's evanescent
proof. The trees, ungreened, starkly tree.
You would have been born in winter.
A dream I dream in the quiet

season of true, absolute night.
I saw you—brief as snow starting
to vanish before it arrives.
You would have been born in winter.

HERE THERE IS NO LANGUAGE

after Jean Valentine

skycurst mind writ
pleas   ink'd birdtalk
goddoctor spoke   deathlike   want I'll
flee   can't can't
ask rope
or step

into dark *go*   *low L—*   *closedown*

PERSEPHONE

after Louise Glück

There was, in you, this coldness.
It turned me cold. My heart,
those days,
like a window left open.

◆

I turned cold. My heart
pointless as stars
above a window. You left
to be good

to me. It was pointless.
The injury was there.
What good were you
to me gone?

Another injury,
like the first
that formed me. It's never gone.
That harm delivered me to you.

◆

First
you touched me, then
the earth opened. Like harm
in the mind, snow

touched everything there
was to be touched. World
bright and unspeaking. Like you. I didn't mind.
That doorway: I climbed in.

◆

The world could not touch me;
I was in the other world.
One with no doors, only windows
to look upon rows of barren trees.

I was in the other world;
my companions were light and silence
I couldn't bear. *Look,* said my mind
as it disappeared.

Only light and silence
left in the field. Snow
my body disappeared
bit by bit.

My back against the snow in the field.
Stripped to the self.
Red, bit by cold. And you
turning, then, cold again. Away.

♦

Suffering stripped me to my self, my true nature
unearthed. A violent kind
of knowing. The world turned cold again, away again
from my mind. There is lucidity

in winter. A necessary violence against the earth.
Loving you was like that.
My heart destroyed, my mind.
To know it could be, and still go on.

Being loved, by you, I
thought would rescue me.
To know someone could
if not myself. This ridiculous

truth. I was not rescued
from suffering; love was suffering
I made myself. Ridiculous,
I abandon the world, return again

to the cleft in the earth. To love, to suffering,
those private days of winter.
I would give it back. The world. *Do not abandon me.*
I speak to the nothing where you are. The scar. In me. This coldness.

FOR LOVE,

after Jean Valentine

I tame my loose upset
I dote you mess me walk away

teethe on my pain   oh oh (tut)
touch   blue   tragedytorn
bleat poetic   ungodly   out (tut)

I writhe that thought   cede bad bad
I detach thought ugh habit

O I'm our sky in the well
stormy   ruinate   ripple

THE THIRTIETH YEAR

after Lucille Clifton

I had expected
to be an ordinary woman.
Dreamed of daughters, beauty, life made
whole by them. Then
the year of losing came, the year I died,
like the trees, again and again.
My sadness plain and always.
A shining blackness in the mind.
I was and was and being
became harder. And I lived
(as if it were ordinary)
years like this.

IF IT MUST BE WINTER, LET IT BE ABSOLUTELY WINTER

after Linda Gregg

Let it be witness. Wolf. Rime bite, brutal tenuity.
Let it be awe. Briefly. Brume—let it twist into sun.
Let it be infinite. Ultimate. Worry, wet, but bless
it. Let snow illume. Renew. Beatify. Trust it. Be bit
by. Beast of it. Bruin. Wren. Ewe. Let it mute. It still.
Nimbus. Let winter obliterate, but sweetly. If it
wails, let it be. Tristful. Numb. Woe-bitten ire. Yet
useful. Interiorly. Sweetbite want. Melt. Bit, bit.
Belief. Wan sun. Let it out. It be wrest. Brittle my I.
Let it blunt me. Wait. (Write it.) Be fruitless. Ebony
tree lit by snow. Mist. Winter. Let it be beautiful.
Wistful. Between its turmoil. (*Baby.*) Enter. I let it
in, in. To try. Let it be awful, bittersweet, sublime.

ON THIS NIGHT IN THIS WORLD

after Alejandra Pizarnik

On this night, in this world,
this familiar unknowing. I write into
night, to bare myself—as one trusts a mirror
in the dark. I have lived a death inside
this silence. Only on the threshold of dream, language, the interior
world, unlocks. A seam of light under a shut door.

IN THE SELF A SILENCE

a cento

In the cave of the self the light shines only so far. I try so hard to be in the world. See only myself in the mirror of. Green night, divining. A constant daydream—which life. Interrupts. Sorrow behind, sorrow ahead. Sorrow. Without end. My self is. No sanctuary. I lost the earth and the flowers of the earth. I lost my life without death. I tired of honest things. It hurt like glass. It hurt like self. Now, if anything touches me, I am ashes. And I, I as I, try as hard as I can try not to be. Between the "I" and the "me," rain. Heavy as August. Windows open on a world I have no language for. The impossible closes. Around like a smooth lake. The sun moves like a ghost. There are sights I see and sounds I hear. Which ripple me. At the pond, green. And again green. And again. Inside I look for the mother. A point where I can see no further. Someone goes into the silence and abandons me. I am as far away as I can be. In myself. I am aware of this. The stillness gives. An edge to the shadows. This shadow here. I am. Wound I long to wound. Dazed shadow of the self. As it follows the self. A witness of the buried life. A message from a secret self. Like a bird I don't expect to see in the rain. My sentences like cries strung together. I am alone. Alone. With language and without meaning. Sometimes it's too hard. With words. Or dark or silence. My last defense is the present tense. Memory stings the brain. Brazen, and before. That difficult. At the edge of what I do not explain a light shines. A slit of light at no-bird dawn. It is a silence made more actual. What does it mean if I say this, years later? I must suffer everything twice. Like a face in a river. Half of me is drowned. Half of me is. Light, I let myself, unresisting, be swallowed. So that I might hear the unsaid. More, clearly. A river. Losing all but its sound. Language of a lost other. World. A world I lose by waking up. Something quieter than sleep. I imagine it— the story that exists. I'm speaking. I speak. Like this.

REMEMBER GREEN'S YOUR COLOR

after Gwendolyn Brooks

Hours long and hushed as graves
in the barren season. Only night can grow.
A season I listened to no
sound, willing the nothing to speak. Shielded my green,
unyielding hurt. I believed that,
if I relinquished the pain of losing you,
I would truly lose you. But pain is fruitless and suffering can
never be your name. You were spring. These bare boughs bloom with song, still of use.

THE MOMENT WHEN A FEELING ENTERS

after Adrienne Rich

the body
is political. Speaking true the body's

suffering made for me a life.
A house. Marzipan. Doctors who see my body

clear. But I don't like the heavy feeling
of their eyes. Under them I flatten. I close. My mind thinks the body

difficult, so mostly it floats. Half terror,
half beauty, like a ghost. In the body

of night, every night, the absence of me
grows dark as pupils. My body

rises into dream where it can't be
touched—and I'm air, rootless, everything and nobody.

◆

I thought, I thought, and wrote
it down. I thought the writing

would change something; it changed
myself. Which, again, I write.

At the edge of sleep, I knock on the night
to let me in. To reach into, under, my self. To write

the true, forbidden thing I do not know
I know. I see only black; I watch it spark. I write

what the dark makes audible. A dream speaking
what's inner. Dark as ink in which it is written.

◆

Pain made me forget
most things. Mostly my self. Blue, I forgot

to look for, filling the trees. Clouds. Flowers
parading along the pavement. I forgot

dew and dawn and the wind
making language of the grass, forgot

leaves, the gauze of early light under,
and spiders, floating, their webs like seams of air. All forgotten—

keys, instructions, years gone, days sliding
into days like water the sea. Pain made me forget

I go on living. Deathtouched, changed, but my life arrives again
at *yet*. It's May. I wake to it, thick and sweet as honey I'd forgotten.

LIVING

after C.D. Wright

If Wednesday, the doctor's. Trees stationed, canceling the first light.

If Wednesday, blue of no privacy.

Boston hospital where in me we see. The overwhelming matter. The whole mind.

Return to my street, the cold season. Eating in my coat without sitting. A tomato, some bread. No green around. Maybe yellow.

Call the doctor. Make a payment.

Call the doctor. Another.

Call the beloved and be mean, to incite feeling.

Write. Into the marrow.

Call the beloved. Tell him what is needed. A suit. Zucchini. Books returned to the library, the ones most hated. Don't share the difficult news. Tell him about the poet canceled most recently, the high school friend's divorce, the latest on war in the east. What's seen—a box of sky, trees with nothing in them.

Leak. Change. The mirror makes a picture that isn't.

Take out the trash. In the mail. On my phone, read an email from a magazine wanting a form, an email from a magazine wanting a form, an email from a magazine about the newest issue, an email about a bargain for things I don't need, an email asking to save the environment as if I could. An email telling me it's time for a change.

Write. Looking long makes a thing strange.

Beat the blanket clean.

Meet students at the college to talk about poetry. Walk there, never pay for parking. Anyone who sees will see a woman living. There is evidence. Everything keeps happening. The students will be standing outside my office. They will smile, collectively, as I walk in, seeing the woman they will learn from, as if happy it's me.

Like daughters. In flannel shirts, naked kneed. Turning, their minds, their rings around long fingers.

Preach about hope. Preach about dream work, what's under. Preach about the split line, how it can mean two things at one time. Imagine the point in the air, where what was is and what will be, too, the nearly after. Preach about form as night comes on.

If Wednesday, wrap it up. The being is done.

If Wednesday, walk home. In the night. Everything becomes night. See the nothing of it whole. Walking, forget the years of never, all that horrible trying. The cold is clear and probable. The light is another's, falling onto the sidewalk. Or planetary. Arriving. The smell of the grass.

DIVINE

A KIND OF DREAMING

A field of poppies bobbing
like pigeons.
The dove-colored rain.

It is a kind of dreaming: how I rehearse
my life.

Pear sliver of moon.
Leaves tumbling in its glow
like white plates.

Only later did it become something real.

I TOO WAS WORTHY

of love. An indestructible
childhood.

I am certain
all this time
God was missing

me. Desperate for
my attention, sent one after
another spectacular catastrophe.

I thought it would never end
and it didn't. I'm going to live

until I don't, whatever I do.

TESTIMONY

Always there was some bleeding,
nobody inside me. My fury
shining. Hyaline silence. A mirror
the color of ice. God
improbable, like time in a dream.
Blame and a surplus of tomorrows
exactly like today. There was so much
nothing. Tracks holding shadow in the snow.

EQUINOX

A dream can kill you.
Blood streaming from
me not equal to its loss.
I've never possessed the faith required.
My future holds
no promise of green.
The wind in the tree
a negative thing.
I was there as the body of
leaves, for a moment, lifted
like a voice at the end
of weeping, like a question
after a door closes.

BETWEEN THE STORIES OF LIVING

The poplars are still
white. Rabbits beneath
like weakness
I do not notice.
The daylight is
clear, the cold
obvious and fragile.
In winter, my presence
stings. There I am,
silent as any woman
in pain. Like any woman,
I live between
the stories of living I tell.
There I am, waiting
in the yard for the occasional
troubling of finches, evanescent songs
of children. All that isn't
mine wilds me.
I can say it now.
The light is clear
and there are no flowers in the garden.

AGAIN THE CHOIRS

Nothing is lost. God
a moment, then

away. Great gray
dissembler.

I was and was
not in the field alone.

Grass
and grass beyond.

The passing world
where this happened.

ONCE I WAS BEAUTIFUL NOW I AM MYSELF

I was much and no one
thought precious. When I cried,
it was a small event.
I never spoke a word; silence
spoke for me. My pills
were white and summer
yellow. Mood smooth
as a shorn lamb. As the days
slipped, my shadow
slendered until no longer
solely mine. Thought the mirror was
a portrait, I sat so still.

POSTCARD

A blur of blossoms. Bougainvillea. On the hill,
someone despairs. Shadowless, beyond
audience. The immaculate
sun unbearable, a supernal
tyrant. I will never know the kind
of pain others endure. But
I have glimpsed the dirt road down
to the sea, the abrupt emptiness.

WHILE LIVING

I arrived here.
How many men have

touched me, fixed me
with a common panic?

Foxglove
in the meadow. Stars

softened like crumbs
of wax. Amazing,

my ordinary weaknesses.
How infinite. How ordinary

to survive them, to be
in the plain evening

speaking of it.

WHAT ARE WE TO DO

I try to hold you
here; my language sours.

You look
past my joy,

oppose it. You insist on
your dramatic

unraveling, love's
souvenir. Living without

you all this
time astonishes me.

I wanted a little more
disaster, to mark

the boundary.
My liminal anguish. Perennial gone.

There is nothing left to worship.

POSTCARD

The mountains hazy behind everything,
like one's knowledge of death.
Crows tossed like stones
into the wind. The hours
ochre, the river
light. More sky
here than anywhere,
songless as a church by the road.

THE VANISHED ROAD, THE MOUNTAIN

on the other side of darkness.
The long blessing

of tide. Night
of jasmine and brine.

Elsewhere, death,
like sunlight,

clarifies a room.

BRUTAL BEAUTY

of the morning. Green window
full of boys
passing, birds
embroidered in the stark
branches. The sun the blue's
singed vacancy. And the sea, of course.
Shattering. Against every body
into light.

POSTCARD

Sky of new snow open
like eternity. Numinous, benign. All
day wind moves the day
along. January still
blank as if unbegun. I've come to face it—
I have to live and go on
living. With the knowledge
oblivion excludes me, apart from
brief, fathomless sleep. This unshakable quiet
I am told is peace. For you,
I count the blessings
which stitch me to this earth. Lacework
of rime. Pines feathered and faithful as swans.
This morning, I woke
and pain, a while, stayed dreaming.
Children unknowable to me
left before my seeing
angels in the yard.

A BLESSING

A blessing: alive!

I see myself
unrecognizable, ice-clear.

I unlock my mouth
for almonds, bells.

Whatever is dead
does not touch me.

Sweet of my own
name on my tongue.

Bewildering, this love
I learn from myself

like a secret in a dream.

THE VISIBLE WORLD

Lilac willing to be beautiful. Wild
blackberries, wild lack—now my tenderness is full
of briars. The light like velvet.
It was a time in the world.
The bluey lake dimming, the rhubarb.
You know—that simple.
Despite everything, there is still a self in me
who worships the visible world
and doesn't take it back.
Egrets. Milkweed. Milk.
I am being here, right now.

NIGHT POEMS

I DREAMED I FORGOT

I dreamed I forgot
who I was—the last woman
to love you. You knew me
as a girl, when joy was
edgeless, and required
no work. Cinquefoil
in the field, our knees
green. In the dream I was
laughing, I watched it
happen. My face marked
by pleasure, changed
to accommodate it.
Myself a little
ugly, this ugliness honest.
And because you were not
there, there was no consequence
and I was glad.

NIGHT POEM

I suffered. It's difficult
to prove. Days of clouds, clouds
like swans, pitiless, mercurial.
Blame the lake. Landscape
so flat I could look into the future.
A year I eyed your narrow hands.
I am trying to tell you how it was.

I CAN'T HELP MYSELF

My body concerns
itself with melodrama and ache, vulgar
wakefulness. Little has changed since
I was first the target of a wrenching
affection. I am not sorry
for having once been young
and no longer. This need
I sharpen like a blade.

A STORY NOW

Love did not make me well: I faded
like a landscape
under intensity of focus.
I am comforted by my grief, as it
confirms the harm. I think what I want
is a story now, from here on out.
A story of a man without the man. Understand:
If it was love, it never saved me.
Freed, I can be wounded
as everyone is, by being
alive—not especially, and all my life
spared insufficient apology.

NIGHT POEM

Beyond the window
God, eternity, snow
glow of the pines
like wraiths against the dark.
Death, I think, and then
I say. I feel
both pain and memory
of pain and struggle
to tell them apart.
It's everywhere, isn't it? That
which would wound me.

IMMODERATE LOVE

You know what doesn't need?
Stones

apart from the moon, its desperate tug

The dark

God

and what a miserable life

He must lead
with nothing to need
and no one to give it to Him

MY SENTIMENTAL AFTERNOON

Around me, the stubborn trees. Here
I was sad and not sad, I looked up
at a caravan of clouds. Will you ever
speak to me again, beyond
my nightly resurrections? My desire
displaces, is displaced. The sun
unrolls black shadows
which halve me. I stand
very still so as not to startle
the song in the branches.
It's true: I am learning to believe
there are beautiful things
never meant for me.

ANGELS

I didn't expect angels, but
they kept coming. A flicker
in the street's margin of shadow.
A mote of gold particulate
pirouetting by the window.
I asked them *can you tell me—am I good?*
but they had little authority.
Useless, really, angels—all aureate
mist and feathers and supererogatory
patience. But I can't abandon them
to terrestrial cruelty. When they arrive, newly
individual and foolish, I
pour them cool water from a pitcher, I offer
blackberries and white cheese. Needless
though they are, on bright mornings
when they stay sleeping (like children; their faces
I decide are mine)—I keep the curtains closed
against the obliterated sky.

CLOSE

I loved you, it didn't make sense.
I dismantled the sanctuary. I convened
my body, then used it
for transit. When you kissed me,
my grief was legible. Your hand
on my neck. Your face close enough at last
to grasp its vacancy.

GOATSONG

I will survive the wrong
I've done. All the love
that didn't serve me.
My youth used up
worshipping mercurial
myopics. I've cried a lot
very briefly. This sorrow has helped
make my career. Yes,
I'm a difficult person
to endure, I hardly manage.
Oh hum, the rest of my life
keeps coming. It feels just
like I knew it would.

AUTUMN

Her crying unfinished
but the day forged on, requiring her
ordinary labor. The cat
with its innocent hunger.
Trash festering below the sink.
She listened for some proof
she was loved, but God was busy
not existing. Then she looked awhile
at the sun through the tree
through the window, otherwise
unframed. Well, not the sun
but the light she understood
as the sun, as so often she confused
something's origin with its consequence—and she thought
this substitution might reveal something
important about her, then
she thought there might be nothing important
about her, and a little
residual feeling welled up
and whatever it was kept shining shining shining.

LOVE OPENS

a door, promises
shelter.
It wants to know
who you've vanished into
like the night shushing
as it parts a field.
It follows you like a moon,
without urgency.
Says things
will be more
or less as expected, for once.
Gifts you
jasmine, peaches
sweeter at the bruise.

NIGHT POEM

Your body diminished
at my touch. It hurt, though
who I'm not sure.
Don't stop loving me
I said, being brave.
But it was a dream—love,
and my speaking of it.

in the black tree more black

the night my I begins a glimpse of endlessness

everywhere the night the night everywhere

moonglimpse by which I see

night silence which repeats itself

to enter the self is to interrupt what is silent

to enter the night is to interrupt what is whole

night which is self which is

nightsnow lays the sky down

in the world of night night unwords the world

in this world both feet my mind the other one

mind of snow body of night

through the dark more dark is

good is dark is night self always speaking under

like God the dark silent perfect always near

nightseeing through my I

trees shadowless or all shadow

dark the night enters dark opening like eyes

dark of my eyes opening to see the dark enter

shadow made of world

dark like God begins its own origin

world vanishes when dreaming my eyes open

dream world I wake to see myself see in clear

I begin when the dream does

moonshadow on nightsnow

night falls like snow on snow a thousand silences

nightworld waking to the dream of its shadow

moon like snow waits to be seen

night I write until it is gone

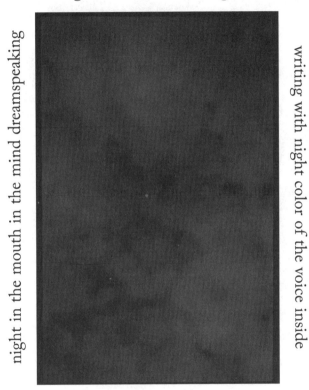

writing with night color of the voice inside

night in the mouth in the mind dreamspeaking

self I write until I appear

I DREAMED

There were no deaths: just sleep.
The sky darkening then undarkening,
and between, so many stars.
Loneliness was a survivable ailment and passed
clear as winter. Fear gone from my ribs.
Whatever was prayed for was
given back. The moon shining
immodestly like the face of a beautiful girl
who knew it. The sky breaking open to reveal
more sky—never the end.

ANGELS ORDINARY

in heaven, birds
of milk. Nightsnow
on the flowers. Allowed no
shadow. The moony
hours. Speaking
their small voices.
Eager in their chaste
tenderness. Ignorant
of sorrow, they laugh
and laugh or else
stay silent. Seam
of gold on night's hem.

NIGHT POEM

The wind gossips,
though most everything stays
sleeping, the stars in the black pouch
of heaven, stones, the unexceptional
foliage, poor wind
with so much to say
and no one to say it to.

A WOMAN HAS TO LIVE HER LIFE

I go to a grave, it isn't yours.
Women who loved the one turned to
ashes poured the ashes
into concrete, made a shrine, said *let's see
anyone take him from us.*
You took you from us
and two decades later I'm on a mountain
startling at butterflies, shivery
phantoms in the yellow clover.
And the clouds quietly knit over.
And I take a different path back down.

GHOSTS

The escape formal,
like a signature.

At a distance

almost lovely—a curtain
through a window, a balloon in a tree.

WATERCOLOR: DRIVING, AWAY

The clouds lay their gray bellies low
A peachy glow filters through
In the fields, yellow
along the top, incidental
Green over green over green
which becomes black, in slow degrees

GRIEF

Like a hawk, gyring
out of reach.
Its sweep of shadow
larger than its origin.
Its inscrutable silences.
How it would lift
then hover, and where
it was, that long, no light
shone through.

I SEE IN MYSELF

a little soul like silk.
Classic and silent.
Silver like a childhood
moon. Who's
my I? I exist
in idiolect,
approximation. Often
I forget my specifics.
I determine a myth,
then settle in.

ONCE IN A WHILE I AM REMINDED

I am not at the center of anything. Seen at a distance
I am hardly seen. Excruciating, how *here*
I am, how little
it means. I use my mouth to make sounds
which approximate my innermost thoughts
but often bungle it. I use my eyes when I need to
be understood. Sometimes I tell the truth
but only when I think I'll be valued
for being interesting instead of good.
I marvel at what I call my life—ambulances, sparrows,
clouds passing definitively by—amazed that it doesn't
know it's mine at all, the minor characters
don't look up, the narrative sags, and I
each moment wondering if this is
when the real story starts.

NIGHT POEM

Violet mountain pressing up
the night. Two lanes and the moon
a distant bright. Miles
of yellow stitch. No cows
in sight. No anyone
but each other.

I DREAMED I FORGOT

I dreamed I forgot you
but to dream you was remembering.
I have words for you
only, a linguistic fidelity.
Cherish and *anguish* and *fool.*
I look for you, I am finding
out if I am brave. Last
I saw you, it was the same disruptive
season: robins trilling in the young
flush, trees shivering
pink all down the street.
I thought the ache
would ruin me, and maybe it did.
Here I am in the beatific after
still calling back to you.

ANNIVERSARY

Sunflowers
by the roadside, mountains
lavender beyond.
Crickets pinkylong
vault into the tall grass.
A cat mewing her unknowable
melancholy from the shade.
I'm looking closely
because I'm alive.
I claim each thing
gift, gift, gift.

SPRING

Green settled, became a bit of happiness.
An hour of sun
polished the branches.
I have devoted myself
to what can be seen, it saves me
some bereavement.
Stones quivering by the roadside.
Bluish milk in a bowl.
Before the house, magnolias
softening like snow.

AFTER THOUGHT

AND WHATEVER I HELD INSIDE ME

burst.
And I could not breathe
in the proper cadence.
And I hissed like I was punctured.
And when I spoke no one heard me.
And I made a mistake
thinking I was finished
with feeling; from behind that partition
surged more than before.
And I choked and nearly vomited on the carpet, like an animal.
And I was deranged, the cat was afraid
and felt pity for me. And I was so sad
now about everything. And I was bewildered
by the novelty of my suffering—
I thought we were well
acquainted—and what it revealed I feared
was the real me, hiding all that time,
who I would be forever after, the self
I would die with, and maybe soon,
I was certain I was breaking open
and whatever remained would be exposed
as irremediable.
And the world was narrowing to a point.
And I closed my eyes so I wouldn't see it.
And the specter of my voice said *Feelings
go in the box! Feelings go in the box!*
And my mind conjured the box.
And I saw it
and obediently I put them in.
And the furniture stayed very still, as if holding its breath.

BRIEF RESPITE IN MID-DECEMBER

there is a little winter light it goes a long way

golden capsule in an upturned palm

cheeks pressed against the knees and deep

breaths breaths counted one two three

outside the world that isn't

particularly concerned about keeping me

leaving like a child

its white sun blue cold all over the place

snow like paperwhites in the window

I could disappear no one would know

the promising thing is that I didn't

what passes for joy: alive

I washed my face and did the dishes

ON PAIN

        The dream of me entered
again and again and left more or less.
Intact. In order. To endure. My body
mined. My mind.

AT THE END

It was a winter, that silence.
Memory, white, and all around
the walls appeared. Beyond
the window, trees, whose
emptiness I trusted.
Myself a figure
of accommodation. Faithful
to the idea of love, the fact
of suffering. Between us, only
cold, shining, like a breath
we shared, common.

JANUARY

Snow cracked beneath

our feet like glass.
Your beauty agony

prepared me for.
The meantime

blue. To touch
then release

your mouth was an achievement.
Silence lucid. The trees.

We lay in cold
our bodies

vanished.

WINTER STREET

Watched a hawk drop from a tree, stumble, fly away,
a little death in its mouth.
Watched the dark as it darkened. Myself
vanishing. The whole time.

FOR THE BABY THAT IS NOT, IS NO LONGER, COULD ONE DAY BE

I swallow capsules the color of loss
in the stilldark morning. I run under water
a fistful of blueberries, a kettle
I watch until it shrieks. My face,
so I can face it. Dutifully
I walk, for my health, my heart, to the room
where I guide others to language
that feels most strange and true.
I decipher the ambiguous
image. I say the unsayable
thing. I lay bare
my disorder in order
to pay for the doctor
who turns the wand slowly,
brow furrowed at the screen.

ON THE BORDER OF LANGUAGE

All my being

                waits. There is no end to

                                night—everywhere

I look, it's there. Absence

                                        opaque. Beneath.

I vigil

                    the dark to hear

                                  some sign of me.

       Sealed inside, I

                                          see a silence

              rage. Black wind

                            in the black trees.

DRIVING UP THE MOUNTAIN

The river swollen because the earth
is different now, has suffered long
damage. I take part in this and no pride,
my new car weaving needlessly down and back
up the mountain so I might have
a particular kind of cheese, sweet
lemons. It's the last summer of my twenties
and I am old enough to feel bad
about everything, if given
the chance. My thighs
thick against the seats, unshaven.
My hair and face unwashed
for days. I speak cruelly
without due prompting
at the tourists slowing down, pulling off
onto the narrow shoulder and running across
for a look. Along the one
road to town, there are petals
flimsy as paper, wings
pitched like litter on the breeze.
It's not that I don't know
what's beautiful, it's just beauty never ends
up the point. I start and stop. I wait. In the back seat,
my eggs rattle, my perishables
grow soft. Peripheral, the river,
silver. Sun riven over water. A girl
leaning precipitously against the rail.

SEASIDE

Dune grasses white and sky
and ocean a massive blackness.
When I am most hurt,
this is how I see the world,
monochrome, the contrast turned
way up. I suppose I am
a little wounded now, by the dream
of the ultrasound, the black
screen and white wand revealing
only more bad news. I'd be fine never
to enter again my interior. Its stark, ruined
topography like the moon
desperately probed for life. I've tried.
Years. To change my suffering, my ways
of seeing it. My failures in this
have made my career, have brought me
here. You can hear the roar
with the door open, which I've done.

ON LOSS

When the   stopped. When
the   vanished. Like a dream—the violence of
its ending, the absence of narrative. There was no
language. In the body, the mind, a mouth. Agape. I
tried to write and every word foundered. Agony—
I saw it. The dark inside, which I was and was
not. The   undone undid me. All night
the leaving came.

NOTHING MAJOR TO REPORT

Only temporary peril—another Thursday.
Blood remains primarily
inside my body. The scream of
the animal is for attention.
Abruptly my shadow reminds
me I am human, in the room,
though the darkness I make
on the walls could be mistaken for storm.
The coulisses of trees endure,
despite my failures to see them
as more than symbol.
The gray seems personal.
The news, sempiternal.
I am of and in an uncertain age.
A coolness descends. The future.

MADTOWN

Who do you think you are?
More often, I'm not sure, though
the voice keeps asking me.
I tread carefully as if I were
a lake and the world without
feeling the bright inscrutable
expanse of winter. I crack
my skin like the blue skin
of the surface, I blink
and, looking down, see the blur of myself
entombed in ice, and the dark beneath
without bottom.

    ◆

T. says she can't stop writing
long poems. She wants to take up space.
And, hearing her say this, I nod my head
as if I, too, felt this, I who want to feel everything
T. feels, so certain in her
suits, her smile glinting like a gun
she is quicker to draw.
But the truth is I've had trouble
feeling much of anything. I don't
say this, as I have as of late said
less and less, perhaps because I'm afraid
I've done too much of both—
feeling and speaking—in the years
preceding this moment, this small moment
of my small life where I nod my head at my friend,
a gag of shadow clamped in my mouth.

    ◆

Who am I? Who am I? Who am I
to take up space? I lie
all day in the coincidental field
of light plotted on my bed. I do not move
to follow it. I stay
buried in sheets sullied
by my continued presence. Hours
pass like strangers—
they have their own concerns,
places to be. I know the world exists
outside, vast and possible,
which exhausts me. Here,
I see the same corner
of roof just outside my window. Sometimes there
is snow, sometimes more or less. I
strip before it but I'm neither
brave nor coy. I'm invisible,
up where no one thinks
to see me, where I stare into the mirror
some nights, uncertain
just who it is I'm looking at.

◆

G. comes, we make
maps, we make
boats, I'm sad (of course)
and when
we take the ancient
poem and make
what we can make
of it, I write
at the top *Grief-*
Farer, the sea
I chart, endless
sea, frozen sea, here
not a sea but a lake
and another, and everything
so still and enormous I
can't stand it.

◆

Blue
sapped away and left
in its place monochrome
boxes of sky.

When I rest
my cheek against
the glass, the chill
seeps into me.

◆

Grief-Farer

I have suffered
grim sorrow. My heart
seethed—a hunger.
I heard nothing
but the roaring. A swan,
an ice-cold wave.
I took to myself and the voice
spoke, icy-feathered. No comfort.
The joys of life far from this.
Terrible, I have had to endure
myself. The shadows darkened,
and now my spirit twists
out of my breast. Fleeting
pleasure, to tear out the life.
There are no angels with which to live
forever and ever.
A fool is the one who comes unprepared.

◆

Weekly, I pay to be listened to. I suppose
this means I believe, despite
myself, I have something
that needs to be said. I am allowed
fifty minutes, on the dot, except with the psychiatrist,
who keeps it short. Truthfully, I'm not sure
he even listens, so it's likely for the best.
I have this *thing* about speaking
and not being

heard. Like most women. A fume
of rage rising where language should
be, eclipsing language, eclipsing
me. And while he doesn't
listen, he certainly watches. And my rage is
an obvious kind, and would be, of course,
written down. So it's likely
for the best.

◆

I write poems.
I stop writing
poems. I stay
up. I sleep
in. In
a lemony
journal I
observe. My
symptoms. The
world.
As I see it.
From my
room. I don't
leave. I eat
—what
do I eat?

I forget.
I forget.
To keep myself,
I write things
down, I hate
every bit of it.

◆

What would I say if I had
the space to say it?
Likely too much.
Likely I would give
myself away, having such
a tenuous grip.
I think someone else should
take the space reserved for me.
Go on. I'm offering it to you
like a slice of cake
from the whole I'd like to swallow.

◆

I come to see sadness
as unprofessional. And because my profession leads me
to be seen, I decide I am
done with sadness, like a habit
I've kicked. Then, furious, sadness
kicks back.

◆

Wisconsin flattens me
to a proper Midwestern
landscape. I walk to the lake
and back, and a month goes by.
I sustain myself with groceries bought from a store
deemed *festival*, but my spirit remains
austere. There are worse things. I tell T.
what one or all three
of my therapists said that week
about my predicament, which is my life.
We laugh. We're depressed,
well dressed, and we're surviving
the winter. In the gray
room in the gray season, we
discuss gender, desire,
ambition. We grit
our teeth. We have to
believe there is more
life after this.

SHADOW/SELF

AT THIS POINT IN TIME

I have begun eating from dirty dishes and stopped washing my hair, but I have a sneaking suspicion this may be the wellest I've been.

I cried alone yesterday as "Have Yourself a Merry Little Christmas" played on the radio. My sentimentality turned rush hour into a gloaming of fiery stars.

I feel such terrible *tenderness.*

Despite this, my life feels muffled, static, and I am continually surprised when faced with indisputable evidence that it is indeed moving—it is in fact barreling forward, possibly without me.

I feel I am asleep and maundering through a [mundane] dream. I am afraid this simply means I am now an ordinary person.

Sometimes I do take the pills prescribed to me.

I've taken to calling my cat "best friend," as in *You are my best friend in the whole world,* and then burying my face in her fur needfully.

Each night she sits on my chest to watch me unblinking, and a bar of orange streetlight lies upon her. Both keep me up but I don't shift away.

I am increasingly alarmed by smaller and smaller things. I realize I am recoiling from pain. I realize this is reaching an extreme when I cannot bear to even read a headline, when I hide my computer where I can't see it, when I panic on the bus suddenly alerted to the fact of my life, of my living, and must count every building rushing past to keep all my seditious atoms intact.

I am distracted from my work. I am distracted by the enormous task of *bettering myself.* I want, as I always have, to be better. In a journal, I write in majuscule WHAT KIND OF WOMAN DO YOU WANT TO BE? I write a separate list of ways to keep myself alive. I am troubled that this continues to be an issue requiring attention, even in the absence of chaos. On the list, I have written ways to harm myself that are not really harm, such as pinching myself or holding an ice cube in my fist. Verso, a catalogue of minor joys. Banana splits and bubble baths. Looking at animals and children in the park. I have done these things. I have done them with a quiet, crazed desperation, as the volume on my life turns lower, as someone continues turning off the lights.

GHOST ARCHIVE

Like a print in snow where something had been. The trees, by wind, reduced. An invisible thing. How I prefer daymoon because it remains a surprise. Of time now I fail. To keep/track. In a drawer a picture of black. In a box of light on the living goes. All could be mine but isn't. Pain revisited revives. Revises. Nothing said where the pen has bled. Or something important. Then lost in the losing.

IMAGINED PHOTOGRAPHS OF ONE WHO WAS/WAS NOT

in the rain the rain the rain

□

double
exposure—the phantom
of you overlaid
the phantom of me

your beauty!
your beauty!

      (you had
        to see it!)

but an interruption
of sun across

your face erases radiantly
your face

           ☐

black what the eye then saw
with some effort
(in this darkness I know you
are there)

no not ruined still
beautiful
—see
(not nothing)

a little red
on the edge
where light's torn
a way in

like a box
I could keep
you inside of you
rising slowly out of
white as if burning through
a field of ice your face water
color I watched become
become before
my eyes but you were still
(the real
thing) there
(the actual
world) before
my eyes but no no
my eyes were not
I thought enough
to ever preserve you

blurrrrrrrrrrrrrr

summer June party
hat on your head
the day indolent stillgold and you
a breeze

alone moving through it

□

you so much close
you're impossible to see

ON SELF

               In everything, I can't help but read myself, my I exhaustive. My objective never objectivity. It started early. The hunger for language revealed the hunger for self. All those photographs: too small for the burden of my own body, bolstered by pillows with a book in my lap. What did I see in my unknowing? Danger of tipping from the weight of my mind. Which I supersede as the self. Now I fear I will disintegrate without words to limn me. Words as outline and interior. To differentiate from world. Which is everywhere, pushing in.

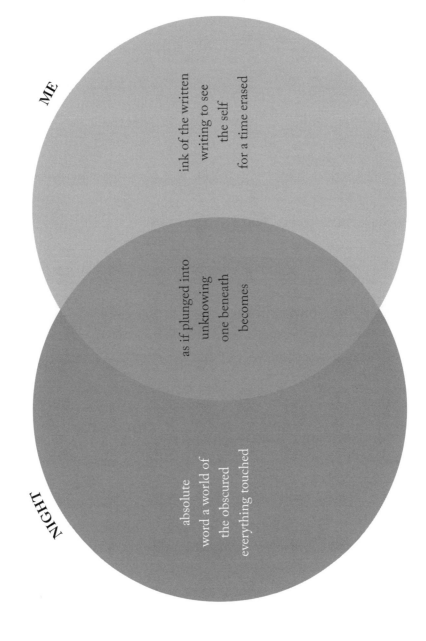

SHADOW/SELF

ME

NIGHT

ink of the written
writing to see
the self
for a time erased

as if plunged into
unknowing
one beneath
becomes

absolute
word a world of
the obscured
everything touched

ARCHAEOLOGIST OF THE DISAPPEARED

I sift through   what remains

black   photographs

of emptiness   distant language

cold and incomprehensible   hours

full of nothing and everything   happened

in the absence of   a witness

I   alone the one

to look   hard

within   glimpse

what was   becoming

as it was   undone

ON SILENCE

I slipped into a silence
like tar. One winter I watched the snow revise
the early night. The dark was obliging, the snow
almost blue. Whatever I said gave me away—
which was nothing. The dark created a space for
my face in the window, in which I saw myself
looking at me as I looked at the night. An image
of knowing: a lightbulb yellow and buzzing,
a wasp encased in glass. (What of me beyond, I
waited for dark to see.) Its opposite: silence,
densest black.

TEA

Five times a day, I make tea. I do this
because I like the warmth in my hands, like the feeling
of self-directed kindness. I'm not used to it—
warmth and kindness, both—so I create my own
when I can. It's easy. You just pour
water into a kettle and turn the knob and listen
for the scream. I do this
five times a day. Sometimes, when I'm pleased,
I let out a little sound. A poet noticed this
and it made me feel I might one day
properly be loved. Because no one is here
to love me, I make tea for myself
and leave the radio playing. I must
remind myself I am here, and do so
by noticing myself: *my feet are cold*
inside my socks, they touch the ground, my stomach
churns, my heart stutters, in my hands I hold
a warmth I make. I come from
a people who pray five times a day
and make tea. I admire the way they do
both. How they drop to the ground
wherever they are. Drop
pine nuts and mint sprigs in a glass.
I think to care for the self
is a kind of prayer. It is a gesture
of devotion toward what is not always beloved
or believed. I do not always believe
in myself, or love myself, I am sure
there are times I am bad or gone
or lying. In another's mouth, *tea* often means gossip,
but sometimes means truth. Despite
the trope, in my experience my people do not lie
for pleasure, or when they should,
even when it might be a gesture

of kindness. But they are kind. If you were
to visit, a woman would bring you
a tray of tea. At any time of day.
My people love tea so much
it was once considered a sickness. Their colonizers
tried, as with any joy, to snuff it out. They feared a love
so strong one might sell or kill their other
loves for leaves and sugar. *Teaism*
sounds like a kind of faith
I'd buy into, a god I wouldn't fear. I think now I truly believe
I wouldn't kill anyone for love,
not even myself—most days
I can barely get out of bed. So I make tea.
I stand at the window while I wait.
My feet are cold and the radio plays its little sounds.
I do the small thing I know how to do
to care for myself. I am trying to notice joy,
which means survive. I do this all day, and then the next.

THE REVERSAL

A man who tries very hard to love me convinces me
to leave, for the first time

in days, my bed, to go outside
to see the frozen lake. And, despite the grandeur of the vast white

field, and the novelty of boys walking across it
like novice deities, I am most interested

in the geese. *Look at them*
sleeping, I say, nodding

to where they rest in a line along the edge of the ice, where the ice is
turning back into water

in imperceptible degrees, the heady blue
encroaching. And I, still

addled by grief, still immoderately exhausted by being
alive, consider (who knows why

my mind does anything it does) how the world could be
flipped—blue lake for blue

sky, birds and feathered
hunks of ice like clouds—

and I think then, naturally, of myself
in this reversal, standing

suddenly atop the firmament,
one of heaven's citizens, perhaps now an angel, perhaps someone

waiting in the long queue
to be seen. And I consider what this would mean

for me, my options. Once, someone
who loved me fiercely fiercely

said *the dead*
have no options, Leila, they're dead! And the angels do nothing

but God's will, loitering in the interminable meantime
useless as pigeons.

Here, the geese sleep at the edge
of the thaw, unbothered. And winter

and the boys forge ahead. And the man goes on
loving me, in the periphery. So I right the earth. I stay there

as long as I can bear, looking at it.

THINGS THE COLOR OF NIGHT

Blackberries. Watermelon seeds. Lunar seas, seen from here. A bruise woken to the day after an injury. The unbroken skin of plums. Unsayable truths in cold authoritative forms. Where the baby isn't in the ultrasound. Eyelashes. Ink. Films when the story is over. Sleep. Crows. Mourning clothes. A beetle's carapace. Licorice. Tar. Teeth rotten through. Tea oversteeped. Olives. Jaguars. The infinite universe. My hair at my birth. Opening in the eye through which I receive the real and exterior world. Anything burned no longer burning. Anything touched by it once it comes.

THE RULES

There will be no stars—the poem has had enough of them. I think we can agree
we no longer believe there is anyone in any poem who is just now realizing

they are dead, so let's stop talking about it. The skies of this poem
are teeming with winged things, and not a single innominate bird.

You're welcome. Here, no monarchs, no moths, no cicadas doing whatever
they do in the trees. If this poem is in summer, punctuating the blue—forgive me,

I forgot, there is no blue in this poem—you'll find the occasional
pelecinid wasp, proposals vaporized and exorbitant, angels looking

as they should. If winter, unsentimental sleet. This poem does not take place
at dawn or dusk or noon or the witching hour or the crescendoing moment

of our own remarkable birth, it is 2:53 in this poem, a Tuesday, and everyone in it is still
at work. This poem has no children; it is trying

to be taken seriously. This poem has no shards, no kittens, no myths or fairy tales,
no pomegranates or rainbows, no ex-boyfriends or manifest lovers, no mothers—God,

no mothers—no God, about which the poem must admit
it's relieved, there is no heart in this poem, no bodily secretions, no body

referred to as *the body,* no one
dies or is dead in this poem, everyone in this poem is alive and pretty

okay with it. This poem will not use the word *beautiful* for it resists
calling a thing what it is. So what

if I'd like to tell you how I walked last night, glad, truly glad, for the first time
in a year, to be breathing, in the cold dark, to see them. The stars, I mean. Oh hell, before

something stops me—I nearly wept on the sidewalk at the sight of them all.

SOMEDAY I'LL LOVE LEILA CHATTI

after Frank O'Hara et al.

Take heart—the lilacs are yours
as much as anyone's; you need never
audition for spring. What delights
delights in you. What is luminous
beckons, and makes room. Look—
there is this goodness
in you that has no debt
and no end. There is this goodness, though
your goodness is not requisite
to stay your while
this side of dirt.
Have you noticed? The stars
do not spell *suffering;*
there's no prophecy in that disorder
of infinite dark, no script.
Misery is not your inheritance.
Your hurt in time will soften
like green beneath
the presence of deer.
If belief's beyond, just be
until it's here. You'll see.
The sacred inside
is not extinguished.
Blood is the mother
of blessing and your veins
run hot with God.
Bless your abundance
of unwieldy feeling! Bless
the holiness of the hole
of your need! Bless, too, this absence
of apology. For your tenderness
is what tethers you

to the exquisite
terrors of living, and living's
all there is. Keep on, keep on.
The smallest voice you have speaks
your most important things.
Are you there?
If you're listening, I think it's all right
to take a breath now. If you're there,
I think it's all right.

I WENT OUT TO HEAR

The sound of quiet. The sky
indigo, steeping
deeper from the top, like tea.
In the absence
of anything else, my own
breathing became obscene.
I heard the beating
of bats' wings before
the air troubled above
my head, turned to look
and saw them gone.
On the surface of the black
lake, a swan and the moon
stayed perfectly
still. I knew this was
a perfect moment.
Which would only hurt me
to remember and never
live again. My God. How lucky to have lived
a life I would die for.

ON NOT WRITING: WILDNESS AS PROCESS AND PROCESSING

For years I felt very bad. There were reasons for it. When asked, as writers often are (at parties, in emails, to fill space), what I was working on, I answered, *Nothing*. This wasn't true, but I felt it was. My project was to stay alive. Which required more effort than I could admit.

The despair began when I finished my first book. Or, rather, it resumed. The book had been something I could throw myself into entire. Writing was an interruption in suffering, a transformation of it; writing about my life gave me an escape from my life. *Entering the poem as a method of leaving the room.*[1]

I was living in Wisconsin, a miserable place to live when you are prone to misery. In Wisconsin it is winter all the time. Even when the glassy lakes thaw back into water, there's this coldness that lingers. It seeps inside. In deep. I think of that time, and a shiver runs through.

I had been brought to Wisconsin to write poems. When the first book closed itself—like a door, final, against me—I thought, *Okay, I will write the next book.* Then The Subjects rushed in. And I thought, *No, not that book.*

◆

I don't want to write the true book; it's the one I want to write: I tear it from myself.[2]

I did not want to write that book, so I stopped writing. But the writing did not stop. It had its own mind, one inside mine.

I did not want to write about The Subjects. I wanted to write about pleasant things, like dogs. If I wrote poems about dogs, then it would be proof I was happy and well-adjusted. But there are certain subjects that, once they're yours, force themselves to the front of the queue. And I did not have a dog. I have a cat, Sylvia, named after exactly whom you think.

I said I'd stopped writing—to you now, and to anyone who asked in those days. What I meant was I'd stopped writing the way I knew how to write, what I recognized as writing, the way I had always written. Before it had been simple, if not easy: I sat at my desk and unstoppered my mind and waited until everything I had to say emptied onto the page, and then the writing was done. It felt good to do it. But this was different—I didn't want to say anything about The Subjects, anything at all. And yet, I had to write poems; poetry paid my rent.

I tried many ways to outrun what there was to say, to shove it down, to go around. But poems are cleverer than the people who write them. And your Subjects—like light, like water, in your hands—ultimately find an opening and slip through.

◆

NIGHT POEMS

What you won't say takes up space. Creates a block. I wanted to say something else, anything else, but the unsaid becomes a stone in the throat.

I believed I could only be a good person (worthy of love and my place on this earth) if I was a good poet, and I believed the way to be a good poet was to write a poem every day. My self-loathing was ouroboric—I felt terrible, so I could not write, and because I did not write, I felt terrible. Obediently I returned to my desk every morning and, all day, obediently I sat in my silence—like a child forced to sit in the mess she's made, as punishment. *I felt very bad.* Then night.

Because I needed to be good, having failed to all day, in bed I would write. On my phone, in the dark. The least I could do was keep my failures organized: one document for each month (for instance, January 2018), in which I would scroll down to an empty space and write into it until I fell asleep. Unthinking (not with my daymind, the one of silence), on the threshold of dream. My only intention was to be accountable, to be good. But it wasn't really writing, I told myself, and whatever had come of it was surely not a poem. *Bad!* Above each one the date, or else: *Night Poem.*

The next day, I vowed, would be different—I would write a real poem, a poem free of suffering, which would then break me free of suffering. Yet each night ended up the same: my finger brushing swiftly against the light so I would not see what, the night prior, my mind had said.

Years I would not look.

◆

That others engaged in dream-near writing was not known to me then. I had never heard of automatism. I did not know of Jung's *most difficult experiment* and had not intended to embark on my own. I wanted only to write. My nightself was porous. Exhaustion wore a hole in me through which the words emerged.

I discovered, in time, other tricks. One was speed. I found that if I wrote very quickly I could get ahead of the censor, the self in me that guarded The Subjects and was terrified that, if I wrote anything at all, The Subjects might spill out. But this trick alone wouldn't do. I couldn't be trusted with freedom, with an infinite range of language (any authoritarian knows this is where the trouble lies). I created a leash and slipped it on. Tethered, at the other end, to a text not my own. Tugging me back. So I could never wander too far into the wilderness.

It worked like this: I would select a book by a poet I admired. Then I would flip very fast, back and forth, through its pages, so fast that my eye and mind could not keep up. I would do this until I snagged on something—not my eye or mind alone, but my whole self. It was a visceral feeling. (Poems are not written only by mind, but inescapably through body.) I recorded these encounters with the text—words, misreadings, associations—and proceeded on, with neither force nor objective. Eventually the poem would finish. On its own terms.

Someone, something gets into you, your hand is an executant, not of you, but of something. Who is it? What, through you, wants to exist.[3]

I came to understand this process as a sort of divining and called it such. As one wanders out into a field, rod in hand, ready for the twitch. I did not know what lay under the surface, but I went out looking, trusting something must be there.

I should note it was during this period that I moved—first from Wisconsin, then frequently. I did my living, briefly, in the Land of Enchantment, in Newbliss, in a room overlooking the sea. In a gray city locals call The Land, but I, sundered, referred to as The Cleave. Detroit. Cincinnati. At the end, on Winter Street.

Bouncing from one place to another, led by poems. And my eye, my mind, my whole self—moving, moving, looking for something to materialize. Somewhere to land.

◆

ORACLE

What, through you, wants to exist.

A child began in me and died in me. And another. And another. And I was, by this, wildly rearranged.

The year I turned thirty, the world upended—the shared one, and my own. The pandemic engendered a new way of living that didn't much feel like living at all. Speaking at a distance, through glass, through shrouds. Forever inside, like specters, shadows against pale boxes of light. Yet we were the ones spared.

I began losing many things. My babies, and then my mind. Track of time and time itself. Touch. My hold on The Subjects, swollen now as a river after a season of heavy, heavy rain.

I have always put my faith in poetry, have come to it for answers. (I have never understood the shame, in poets, in admitting this.) And there was no one else, then, to turn to—the world closed, I lived inside a room of books. This is not metaphor. In place, I sheltered. I lived inside, my inside lined with books. I did this to survive. I did.

So, sequestered in my personal library, wildered by grief, I looked to the poets who had all my life guided me. Those women who, like oracles, spoke the true thing. Godmouthed. Who had seen what was and would be. And said it strange.

Oracle: from the Latin *orare*. To pray or to speak. Surely they lived as I did. Needing to write poems, in order to do both at the same time.

I approached their poems like the prophecies of oracles—something to be deciphered, the message cryptic. The oracle at Delphi was originally a girl, then later a woman over the age of fifty. Her title: Pythia. My mind sees this and instinctively reads it as code, rearranging its letters: **Sylvia Plath.** It was with her work I began, first woman poet I encountered on my way to becoming one. Poet who spoke the unsayable thoughts I could not name and had believed were mine alone.

Poet: from the Greek *poietes.* Maker.

I came back to her poems because I was failing. When my body could not create a child who survived my body, my mind could not create a poem that did. Grief unmakes. The world, the word. Because I approached it desperately, language fled from me. Language is like an animal, wary of fear. Say each word was a bird—alighting briefly, out of reach and then gone again. Or, when caught forcibly, it wrestled fiercely against my grip, then died from the strain of its efforts.

A woman who writes is a woman who dreams about children.[4]

The writing started with Plath's poem "Childless Woman." I took the title and the final word of each line. *Womb, moon, go.* I planted the words on the page and then more sprung up from the depths of me, to fill in the spaces. I wrote into the poem to discover what else it—I—had to say. To forge a way forward.

I continued like that, looking to unearth in poems the message beneath, because I needed there to be a message beneath. My mind sought a cipher. If an answer wasn't clear, it wasn't because an answer wasn't there—surely one existed, in code, waiting to be unlocked. Broken. Language of transformation required transformation of language. It wasn't that I garbled up the poems to make something incomprehensible; it was through these translations that I was able to approach what was wild in me and teach it to speak.

The awareness of disorder generates in the human mind a spontaneous ordering response.[5]

I turned to codes—forms—instinctually, to order what was, in me, disordered. These forms arose organically, order as arrangement as well as command. When reading again the poems that held significant meaning for me, I would sometimes feel an urge. (I had learned by then to listen to my body's somatic interjections.) Then a thought would come: *what happens if I do this:* _____. Then I would do that thing.

One of these earliest codes was what I came to call THE ANTIPODE. I took a poem and translated it, word by word, into its exact opposite as faithfully as I could. *I became you, good* was *bad, day* flipped to *night.* Trauma disorients. It turns what is known into what is unknown. It whelms the self. The world. Upends.

Some words were slippery. What is shadow's shadow side? Is it light, or is it the body between? The antipodes revealed to me how I view what I view, my inner calculations. I developed a double sight—seeing through what was said to what was unsaid, seeing both at the same time. The words inside the word. The refracting lens of the self, translating world. Awful, full of awe.

Antipode: originally *those who have their feet against our feet*—inhabitants on the opposite side of the earth. My feet against the feet of another woman, against language, against the threshold of death. (One of my stipulations: all of the women whose poems I "translated" through code were women who had already passed into that other world, beyond.) Or myself pressed against my other self—my feet rooted in/against shadow. One standing in the world of consciousness, the other submerged. I imagine myself standing on a plane of ice sealing a lake, as a shadow presses, urgently, up, to shatter it from below.

Forms born from wildness, like dreams, create *a space that is both totally free and totally limited.*[6] The disorder was so great that I required greater and greater order. When the brace of the Golden Shovel[7] left too much flexibility for my comfort, I added another, creating THE GOLDEN HINGE: a form in which a borrowed line can be read horizontally as the first line of the poem as well as vertically down the left spine, as the first words of each line.

I wrote poems using only the words of another poem, the original text a word bank. When that wasn't constraint enough, I layered on more form—a pantoum written using only the words of another poem, a ghazal. I tightened it further, writing poems in which each line was an anagram of the original poem's corresponding line (my poem's first line an anagram of the original poem's first line, my poem's second line an anagram of the original poem's second line, etc.). Then I wrote a poem in which every line of the poem was an anagram of a single borrowed line, that borrowed line serving as its title.

Like this, during the worst of it, I learned to write again. My mind taking apart, then remaking. An ear pressed to the wall of the page. Down labyrinthine tunnels of pages, of words, of self. Until I came out the other side.

◆

I speak of form, of lineage, how together these led me back to language, which led me back to living. But it is impossible to speak of lineage of the mind without speaking of lineage of the body and be speaking the truth.

I wanted to die. I say it plain because it is plain; it isn't interesting. My project of staying alive is one passed down. Before me, my aunt and grandmother, and more women beyond. Disorder of the body disordered the mind. I was not the first to lose a baby, to be racked by her efforts toward one. Pattern is order and order is form. If I inherited this form, did I already know the steps to follow—did I already know the way to the end? The women in my family could never be oracles, dead long before fifty. Seers of no future.

Poetry without form is a fiction. But that there is a freedom in words is the larger fact, and in poetry, where formal restrictions can bear down heavily, it is important to remember the cage is never locked.[8]

Form can be a container for pain, but it must never be a prison of pain. If a form no longer suits, break it. Or create another. I can tell you this now: form's gift is not in knowing the end. Form is instruction into greater mystery.

Suicide is the opposite of imagination. The creative impulse is an impulse against death. Inspiration: from the Latin, *inspirare*. To breathe. I never wanted to die—this is, of course, mistranslation. I wanted not death but less pain in my living. And whatever it promised, that vast silence, the desire to create was greater. *Use the hum / of your wound.*[9] Pain made me turn to poetry, and poetry—the art of new seeing, of infinite possibility—returned me to world.

◆

Do you know what I was, how I lived? You know
what despair is; then
winter should have meaning for you.[10]

It is winter as I write this. I have taken breaks to hold my daughter, to nurse her in front of the window I keep unshaded so as to watch the snow. Snow is private. It convinces me I am invisible, though I am clearly seen.

In the years I did not write, I wrote a book. There were reasons. I needed to live, to make, to make a living. To heed the little bit of God in me, the part that creates. Cannot help but to. Thank God.

In time it became easier—my life and the writing of it, the two intertwined. I became braver. I could say things plain, without constraints to hold me. After thought, beyond the shadow. Some of The Subjects were named, which stilled the others.

Again it is winter. What is wild sleeps deep. There are stars of snow in the trees. A cloud rising, then vanishing, above my tea. The writing is done for now. Quiet, but not silent. Here in the room. The world. Milk shining on her cheek.

NOTES

1. Adrienne Rich, "Shooting Script"
2. Hélène Cixous, *Three Steps on the Ladder of Writing*
3. Marina Tsvetaeva, *Art in the Light of Conscience;* quoted in Hélène Cixous, *Three Steps on the Ladder of Writing*
4. Hélène Cixous, *Three Steps on the Ladder of Writing*
5. Gregory Orr, *Poetry as Survival*
6. Hélène Cixous, *Three Steps on the Ladder of Writing*
7. A form by Terrance Hayes
8. C.D. Wright, *Cooling Time*
9. Anne Carson, "First Chaldaic Oracle"
10. Louise Glück, "Snowdrops"

NOTES

The first epigraph is a conversation between Carl Jung and his soul regarding *The Red Book: Liber Novus*, a handwritten, long-unpublished manuscript he worked on between 1914 and 1930. Jung composed this manuscript in the night hours, documenting his "confrontation with the unconscious." In it, he writes, "My soul, where are you? Do you hear me? I speak, I call you—are you there? I have returned, I am here again. . . . This life is the way, the long sought-after way to the unfathomable, which we call divine."

The second epigraph is a line from Alejandra Pizarnik's "The Night, The Poem."

Leila, in Arabic, means *night*.

ORACLE

In this section, I use on occasion a form I've created called the ANTIPODE. This form is written by taking an existing poem and rewriting it using words' opposites. With some words, it is easy to conceive of an opposite (day/night, on/off), but others (owl, dream, glass) require leaps of thought.

I also use a form I call the GOLDEN HINGE—after Terrance Hayes's form the Golden Shovel—in which a borrowed line can be read horizontally as the first line of the poem and vertically down the spine, as the first words of each line.

"In the Night Many Voices" is a cento composed of lines by Etel Adnan, Anna Akhmatova, Margaret Atwood, Lucie Brock-Broido, Anne Carson, Lucille Clifton, H.D., Carolyn Forché, Vievee Francis, Christine Garren, Louise Glück, Linda Gregg, Joy Harjo, Brenda Hillman, Jane Hirshfield, Marie Howe, June Jordan, Jane Kenyon, Dorianne Laux, Edna St. Vincent Millay, Lisel Mueller, Alice Notley, Naomi Shihab Nye, Sharon Olds, Mary Oliver, Alicia Suskin Ostriker, Alejandra Pizarnik, Sylvia Plath, Adélia Prado, Adrienne Rich, Mary Ruefle, Sappho, Anne Sexton, Anita Skeen, Ruth Stone, Mary Szybist, Marina Tsvetaeva, Jean Valentine, and C.D. Wright.

"One Woman" is written as an antipode of sections of Sylvia Plath's poem "Three Women."

"In Lament of My Uterus" is an antipode of the Anne Sexton poem "In Celebration of My Uterus."

"Childless Woman" borrows its title and end words from the Sylvia Plath poem.

"Lost Baby Poem" adapts its title and refrain—"You would have been born in winter"—from the Lucille Clifton poem.

"Here There Is No Language" borrows its title from the Jean Valentine poem. Each line is an anagram of the corresponding line in the original poem.

"Persephone" is written using only (with wiggling) words found in Louise Glück's poem "October."

"For Love," borrows its title from the Jean Valentine poem. Each line is an anagram of the corresponding line in the original poem.

"The Thirtieth Year" adapts, in its first two lines, the last two lines of Lucille Clifton's "the thirty eighth year," and is written using only (with wiggling) words found within the original poem.

"If It Must Be Winter, Let It Be Absolutely Winter" borrows its title from the conclusion of Linda Gregg's poem "Part of Me Wanting Everything to Live." Each line is an anagram of this sentence. "(Write it.)" is a nod to Elizabeth Bishop's poem "One Art."

"On This Night in This World" is a golden hinge written on a line by Alejandra Pizarnik.

"In the Self a Silence" is a cento composed of lines by Etel Adnan, Anna Akhmatova, Margaret Atwood, Lucie Brock-Broido, Gwendolyn Brooks, Anne Carson, Lucille Clifton, Toi Derricotte, Emily Dickinson, Deborah Digges, H.D., Carolyn Forché, Louise Glück, Linda Gregg, Kimiko Hahn, Joy Harjo, Lyn Hejinian, Brenda Hillman, Jane Hirshfield, June Jordan, Jane Kenyon, Dorianne Laux, Denise Levertov, Audre Lorde, Amy Lowell, Bernadette Mayer, Jane Mead, Edna St. Vincent Millay, Lisel Mueller, Lorine Niedecker, Alice Notley, Mary Oliver, Alicia Suskin Ostriker, Alejandra Pizarnik, Sylvia Plath, Adélia Prado, Adrienne Rich, Mary Ruefle, Muriel Rukeyser, Sappho, Anne Sexton, Stevie Smith, Gertrude Stein, Ruth Stone, Anna Swir, Mary Szybist, Marina Tsvetaeva, Jean Valentine, Diane Wakoski, and C.D. Wright.

"Remember Green's Your Color" is a Golden Shovel, borrowing "You are spring," its title, and the line composed by the end words from the Gwendolyn Brooks poem "To the Young Who Want to Die."

"The Moment When a Feeling Enters" is written after Adrienne Rich's "The Blue Ghazals," using only (with a bit of wiggling) words found within it, and borrowing its title/italicized text.

"Living" is written after C.D. Wright's poem "Living," using only words found within it.

DIVINE

All poems in this section were written using a process I call DIVINING. Divining is about opening the self, cognitively and somatically, for influence, and being alert and receptive to what snares your attention. This process involves flipping through the book of another poet very quickly, not reading individual poems but, rather, allowing the eye to fall upon language intuitively, and receiving, without force or objective, words, misreadings, associations, and leaps of imagination, recording as you go along until the poem decides it is finished and pushes you out.

Poems in this section were divined from the following poets:

Margaret Atwood: "What Are We to Do"; "Brutal Beauty"
    "There is nothing left to worship" is an adaptation of a line from "Some Objects of Wood and Stone."

Lucie Brock-Broido: "The Visible World"
    The phrase "worships the visible world" is adapted from the poem "Dear Shadows,." The line "I am being here, right now" is borrowed from the poem "Lucid Interval."

Paul Celan: "Again the Choirs"; "A Blessing"
    "Nothing is lost" is borrowed from the poem "Stretto."

Lucille Clifton: "Testimony"; "Equinox"
     The phrase "always there was some bleeding" is borrowed from the poem
     "brothers."

Linda Gregg: "Between the Stories of Living"
     The phrase "my presence stings" is borrowed from the poem "The Wife."

Joy Harjo: "Postcard" (The mountains hazy)

Jane Kenyon: "Postcard" (Sky of new snow open)
     "I have to live and go on living" is adapted from the poem "Evening Sun."

Galway Kinnell: "Postcard" (A blur of blossoms); "The Vanished Road, the Mountain"
     The phrase "know the kind of pain others endure" is borrowed from the poem
     "The Burn" and the phrase "the abrupt emptiness" is borrowed from "The
     Porcupine." "The vanished road . . . on the other side of darkness" is adapted
     from "Little Sleep's-Head Sprouting Hair in the Moonlight."

Adrienne Rich: "While Living"

Anne Sexton: "A Kind of Dreaming"; "Once I Was Beautiful Now I Am Myself"
     The line "Only later did it become something real" is borrowed from "The
     Breast." The title "Once I Was Beautiful Now I Am Myself" is from "You,
     Doctor Martin."

Franz Wright: "I Too Was Worthy"
     "I too was worthy of love" is a line borrowed from "Will."

NIGHT POEMS

"Examination of Night" is written after Anthony Cody's "Examination of Ruin."

"A Woman Has to Live Her Life" borrows its title from the line "A woman has to live
her life, or live to repent not having lived it" in D.H. Lawrence's *Lady Chatterley's Lover.*

AFTER THOUGHT

"On Pain" and "On Loss" are written after Anne Carson's *Short Talks*.

"On the Border of Language" is borrowed from Alejandra Pizarnik's poem "A Night Shared in a Memory of Escape."

"Madtown": Thanks to Tiana Clark and Gabrielle Calvocoressi, without whom this poem would not exist. This poem also references the Old English poem *The Seafarer*.

SHADOW/SELF

"On Self" and "On Silence" are written after Anne Carson's *Short Talks*.

"Archaeologist of the Disappeared" is written on a line from Billy-Ray Belcourt's "An NDN Boyhood."

"Tea": French psychiatrist Pierre Maréschal claimed in 1937 that all Tunisians were "born addicts," incapable of moderate consumption. He alludes in his paper to "teaism," a medical and psychiatric diagnosis created in the 1920s in Tunisia by the French, which posits that Tunisians' "overconsumption" of tea could lead to hallucinations, psychosis, and murder. Maréschal concluded, "The native is indeed a born addict, but so far he has not yet found his true poison."

"Someday I'll Love Leila Chatti" is written in the lineage of poems by Frank O'Hara ("Katy"), Roger Reeves, and Ocean Vuong.

ACKNOWLEDGMENTS

Poems in this collection have been previously published in the following journals and anthologies:

32 Poems: "Seaside"

Academy of American Poets Poem-a-Day: "The Rules"; "I Went Out to Hear"

Alaska Quarterly Review: "Again the Choirs"; "Night Poem" (I suffered)

Colorado Review: "I See in Myself"; "I Dreamed I Forgot"

The Common: "My Sentimental Afternoon"

The Georgia Review: "Lost Baby Poem"; "Someday I'll Love Leila Chatti"

Gulf Coast Online: "Living"

The Iowa Review: "Brief Respite in Mid-December"

The Journal: "Postcard" (Sky of new snow open); "For the Baby That Is Not, Is No Longer, Could One Day Be"

The Kenyon Review: "The Reversal"

Laurel Review: "Watercolor: Driving, Away"; "Night Poem" (Violet mountain pressing up)

The Massachusetts Review: "Persephone"

Michigan Quarterly Review: "Once I Was Beautiful Now I Am Myself"; "Spring"

The Missouri Review: "And Whatever I Held Inside Me"; "Tea"

The Montreal International Poetry Prize Anthology 2022: "Autumn"

Narrative: "Childless Woman"; "Driving up the Mountain"

New England Review: "In Lament of My Uterus"; "Angels"

Ninth Letter: "Angels Ordinary" (as "Night Poem")

Pleiades: "Testimony"; "Postcard" (The mountains hazy)

Poetry: "Nothing Major to Report"

Poetry Northwest: "I Dreamed"; "Grief"; "Once in a While I Am Reminded"; "January"

The Pushcart Prize XLV: Best of the Small Presses 2021 Edition: "The Rules"

Salamander: "I Dreamed I Forgot"; "Night Poem" (Your body diminished); "Night Poem" (The wind gossips)

Salt Hill Journal: "Immoderate Love"; "Goatsong"

Southeast Review: "On Loss"; "Things the Color of Night"

West Branch: "The Thirtieth Year"; "The Moment When a Feeling Enters"

The Yale Review: "Equinox"

To the many doctors, therapists, and healthcare providers—Dr. Rein and Kate in particular—who have bettered, and so saved, my life: I am grateful every day.

My sincere gratitude to Cleveland State University, the Cleveland Foundation and the Anisfield-Wolf Book Awards, the Helene Wurlitzer Foundation of New Mexico, the University of Cincinnati, Mackinac State Historic Parks, the Kenyon Review Writers Workshops, Smith College and the Boutelle-Day Poetry Center, Pacific University, and the National Endowment for the Arts for their support during the writing of these poems.

Deepest thanks to my editors extraordinaire, Michael Wiegers and Ashley E. Wynter, and to the wonderful team at Copper Canyon Press who make these dreams possible.

Many cheers—and hugs!—to Matt Donovan, Caryl Pagel, Hilary Plum, Michael Deagler, Rebekah Hewitt, and Mag Gabbert for their guidance, enthusiasm, and friendship.

An extra, extra special thank you to Jessica "J.J." Starr, Nathan McClain, and Zora, the greatest encouragers.

Endless gratitude to Felicia Zamora, for her radical imagination, and for believing in what this book—and I—could be.

For my family, blood and chosen (Bryce, Erin, Sam, Tyree, Dorianne, and Joe)—all my love.

I will never be able to say thank you enough to my husband, Aric, and our wonderful cat, Sylvia, for the beautiful life they've built with me, the life that is these poems. And Naïma, my dearest one, for everything to come. For everything you are. I love you, love you, love you, without end.

ABOUT THE AUTHOR

Leila Chatti is a Tunisian-American poet and author of *Deluge* (Copper Canyon Press, 2020), winner of the 2021 Levis Reading Prize, the 2021 Luschei Prize for African Poetry, and longlisted for the 2021 PEN Open Book Award. She is also the author of four chapbooks. Her honors include multiple Pushcart Prizes, grants from the Barbara Deming Memorial Fund and the Helene Wurlitzer Foundation, and fellowships from the National Endowment for the Arts, the Fine Arts Work Center in Provincetown, and Cleveland State University, where she was the inaugural Anisfield-Wolf Fellow in Writing and Publishing. Her poems appear in *The New York Times Magazine, The Nation, The Atlantic, Poetry*, and elsewhere. She is a Provost Fellow at the University of Cincinnati and teaches in Pacific University's low-residency MFA program.

Copper Canyon Press poets are at the center of all our efforts as a nonprofit publisher. Poets create the art of our books, and they read and teach the books we publish. Many are also generous donors who believe in financially supporting the vibrant poetry community of Copper Canyon Press. For decades, our poets have quietly donated their royalties, have contributed their time to our fundraising campaigns, and have made personal donations in support of emerging and established poets. Their generosity has encouraged the innovative risk-taking that sustains and furthers the art form.

The donor-poets who have contributed to the Press since 2023 include:

Jonathan Aaron

Pamela Alexander

Kazim Ali

Ellen Bass

Erin Belieu

Mark Bibbins

Linda Bierds

Sherwin Bitsui

Jaswinder Bolina

Marianne Boruch

Laure-Anne Bosselaar

Cyrus Cassells

Peter Cole and Adina Hoffman

Elizabeth J. Coleman

Shangyang Fang

John Freeman

Forrest Gander

Jenny George

Dan Gerber

Jorie Graham

Roger Greenwald

Robert and Carolyn Hedin

Bob Hicok

Ha Jin

The estate of Jaan Kaplinski

Laura Kasischke

Jennifer L. Knox

Ted Kooser

Stephen Kuusisto

Deborah Landau

Sung-Il Lee

Ben Lerner

Dana Levin

Maurice Manning

Heather McHugh

Jane Miller

Roger Mitchell

Lisa Olstein

Gregory Orr

Eric Pankey

Kevin Prufer

Alicia Rabins

Dean Rader

Paisley Rekdal

James Richardson

Alberto Ríos

David Romtvedt

Sarah Ruhl

Kelli Russell Agodon

Natalie Shapero

Arthur Sze

Yuki Tanaka

Elaine Terranova

Chase Twichell

Ocean Vuong

Connie Wanek

Emily Warn

Poetry is vital to language and living. Since 1972, Copper Canyon Press has published extraordinary poetry from around the world to engage the imaginations and intellects of readers, writers, booksellers, librarians, teachers, students, and donors.

WE ARE GRATEFUL FOR THE MAJOR SUPPORT PROVIDED BY:

academy of american poets

OFFICE OF ARTS & CULTURE
SEATTLE

ARTSFUND

THE PAUL G. ALLEN FAMILY FOUNDATION

Hawthornden Foundation

POETRY FOUNDATION

INGRAM CONTENT GROUP

the point
envision·enact·evolve

MCSWEENEY'S

WASHINGTON STATE ARTS COMMISSION

ART WORKS.

National Endowment for the Arts
arts.gov

The Witter Bynner Foundation for Poetry

TO LEARN MORE ABOUT UNDERWRITING
COPPER CANYON PRESS TITLES,
PLEASE CALL 360-385-4925 EXT. 105

WE ARE GRATEFUL FOR THE MAJOR SUPPORT PROVIDED BY:

Anonymous

Jill Baker and Jeffrey Bishop

Anne and Geoffrey Barker

Mona Baroudi and Patrick
  Whitgrove

Lisha Bian

John Branch

Diana Broze

John R. Cahill

Sarah J. Cavanaugh

Keith Cowan and Linda Walsh

Peter Currie

Geralyn White Dreyfous

The Evans Family

Mimi Gardner Gates

Claire Gribbin

Gull Industries Inc.
  on behalf of William True

Carolyn and Robert Hedin

David and Jane Hibbard

Bruce S. Kahn

Phil Kovacevich and Eric Wechsler

Eric La Brecque

Maureen Lee and Mark Busto

Ellie Mathews and Carl Youngmann
  as The North Press

Kathryn O'Driscoll

Petunia Charitable Fund and
  advisor Elizabeth Hebert

Suzanne Rapp and Mark Hamilton

Adam and Lynn Rauch

Emily and Dan Raymond

Joseph C. Roberts

Cynthia Sears

Kim and Jeff Seely

Tree Swenson

Julia Sze

Donna Wolf

Jamie Wolf

Barbara and Charles Wright

In honor of C.D. Wright
  from Forrest Gander

Caleb Young as C. Young Creative

The dedicated interns and faithful
  volunteers of Copper Canyon Press

The pressmark for Copper Canyon Press
suggests entrance, connection, and interaction
while holding at its center
an attentive, dynamic space for poetry.

This book is set in Adobe Caslon Pro.
Book design by Phil Kovacevich.
Printed on archival-quality paper.